Contents

Welcome

You are so important to the life of the Christian church! You have consented to join with other people of faith who, through the millennia, have sustained the church by extending God's love to others. You have been called and have committed your unique passions, gifts, and abilities to a position of leadership. This Guideline will help you understand the basic elements of that ministry within your own church and within The United Methodist Church.

Called to Spiritual Leadership

Each person is called to ministry by virtue of his or her baptism, and that ministry takes place in all aspects of daily life, in and outside the church. As a pastoral leader or leader among the laity, your ministry is not just a "job," but a spiritual endeavor. You *are* a spiritual leader now, and others will look to you for spiritual leadership. What does this mean?

First, *all* persons who follow Jesus are called to grow spiritually through the practice of various Christian habits (or "means of grace") such as prayer, Bible study, private and corporate worship, acts of service, Christian conferencing, and so on. Jesus taught his disciples practices of spiritual growth and leadership that you, as a disciple, are to share with others as they look to you to be a model and guide.

Second, it means that you always keep your eye on the main reasons for any ministry—to help others grow to a mature faith in God that moves them to action on behalf of others, especially "the least" (see Matthew 25:31-46). This is an aspect of "disciple making," which is the ultimate goal of all that we do in the church.

CULTIVATING VISION AND MISSION

As a spiritual leader, a primary function you carry is to help those you lead to see as clearly as possible what God is calling your church to be and to do. Ideally, your church council first forms this vision and then forms plans and goals for how to fulfill that vision. As a leader, you will help your team remain focused and accountable to honor the vision and goals to which the church is committed. You will help your team create and evaluate suggestions, plans, and activities against the measure: *Does this move us closer to our church's vision to bring others to God in this place and time?*

GUIDELINES

evangelism
Sharing the Good News

Kwasi Kena
General Board of Discipleship

EVANGELISM

Copyright © 2008 by Cokesbury

This book is printed on acid-free paper.

ISBN 978-0-687-64921-1

Some paragraph numbers for and language in the Book of Discipline *may have changed in the 2008 revision, which was published after these Guidelines were printed. We regret any inconvenience.*

MANUFACTURED IN THE UNITED STATES OF AMERICA

CHRISTIAN CONFERENCING

While there are appropriate and useful business-like practices that apply to church life, Christian practices distinguish the church as the church. In the United Methodist tradition, how we meet and work together is important. "Christian Conferencing" involves listening not only to each other, but also listening intently for the will of God in any given task or conversation. This makes prayer essential in the midst of "business as usual." As Christians, we are called to "speak the truth in love." This is a special way to speak in which we treat one another as if each of us were Christ among us. As a spiritual leader in your ministry area, you have the privilege and opportunity to teach and model these practices. By remembering that each of us is beloved of God and discerning the presence of God in all that the church does, every task becomes worshipful work.

THE MISSION OF THE UNITED METHODIST CHURCH

The United Methodist Church is a connectional church, which means in part that every local church is interrelated through the structure and organization of districts, conferences, jurisdictions, and central conferences in the larger "family" of the denomination. *The Book of Discipline of The United Methodist Church* describes, among other things, the ministry of all United Methodist Christians, the essence of servant ministry and leadership, how to organize and accomplish that ministry, and how our connectional structure works (see especially ¶¶125–138).

Our Church is more than a structure; it is a living organism. The *Discipline* describes our mission to proclaim the gospel and to welcome people into the body of Christ, to lead people to a commitment to God through Jesus Christ, to nurture them in Christian living by various means of grace, and to send persons into the world as agents of Jesus Christ (¶122). Thus, through you—and many other Christians—this very relational mission continues.

(For help in addition to this Guideline and the *Book of Discipline*, see "Resources" at the end of your Guideline, www.umc.org, and the other websites listed on the inside back cover.)

Why Evangelism Is Important

You have been chosen to be a leader in your congregation, with responsibility for the ministry area of evangelism. No ministry of the church is more important than reaching people with the good news of Jesus Christ. Without evangelism, the church will cease to exist. A common truism notes that the church is always one generation away from extinction.

Evangelism in the Twenty-first Century

For much of the previous *modern era,* evangelism training stressed knowing the right answers. Questions were considered unnecessary distractions. Questions were the enemy. Skill in precluding questions was once a necessity in witnessing. *To preclude* means *to prevent, to make impossible through some action taken in advance.* The canned presentation method of evangelism with all the prepackaged, *correct* information worked in the modern era.

Then a funny thing happened. We shifted into the *postmodern* or *post-Christian* era. With that era shift came a change in fundamental values, attitudes, and beliefs. The mood of people has changed toward the world and religion. There is no longer a single, universal worldview accepted by all. There is little tolerance for anyone who claims to have a corner on *THE* truth. Questions abound in this new era, and they must not be precluded or discouraged. Any religion that chooses to preclude today's questions is destined to retreat into obsolescence.

The purpose of this Guideline is to offer you concepts and action steps that will help your congregation share their Christian faith in this *twenty-first century context.* The action steps are meant to serve as discussion starters to educate and motivate small groups and the larger congregation to participate in evangelism ministry.

Evangelism—a Three-fold Definition

The aim of the ministry of evangelism is, in short, to relate people to God so that they will begin an initial relationship with Jesus Christ. Evangelism does not end with a person's decision to begin this initial relationship, however. Effective evangelism must lead new Christians into a process of ongoing discipleship and spiritual formation. Evangelism without discipleship often results in *church members* who quickly become inactive.

Evangelism has become a problematic term for some in the twenty-first century. In order to understand evangelism more fully, let's examine the word *evangel*. Just what is the evangel? In the early church, three Greek words described the *evangel*: *euaggelizesthai, marturein,* and *kerussein.* Translated, these three words mean to: (a) tell good news, (b) bear witness, and (c) proclaim.

Tell Good News

What was the good news that Jesus shared? The first evidence of the good news is found in Luke's Gospel where Jesus recites a lesson from Isaiah 61.

> The Spirit of the Lord is upon me, / because he has anointed me to bring good news to the poor. / He has sent me to proclaim release to the captives / and recovery of sight to the blind, / to let the oppressed go free, to proclaim the year of the Lord's favor (Luke 4:18-19).

The year of the Lord's favor, also called Jubilee, represented a forgiveness of past burdens and a fresh start. This passage underscores care and concern for the poor and marginalized people in society. The good news promised relief and release.

Action Step:
Discuss the following with your pastor, leaders, and congregation:
1. What things are we already doing as a congregation to offer relief to people from spiritual, physical, financial, or social burdens?
2. What additional steps might our local church take to help people who need *good news*?
3. List specific ways to share *good news* in our community. Think of things that our congregations actually *can* do. Focus on at least one of the suggestions. Strive to do more than you have been doing in the past.

TWO GOOD NEWS EMPHASES: REPENTANCE AND THE KINGDOM (REIGN) OF GOD

The early church emphasized two key elements of the good news: (1) repentance (turning away from evil and turning to good—through salvation in Jesus Christ) and (2) the announcement of the kingdom of God (God's reign on the earth).

Action Step:
Discuss the following questions with your pastor, leaders, and congregation.
1. How do we talk to people about repentance?

2. The invitation to repent or turn away from evil is still relevant today. Just as in addiction recovery programs, admitting that one is, or has been, participating in evil is the first step toward healing. How do we teach people to resist evil and live better lives?
3. What testimony of repentance can we share individually with others from our personal walk with Jesus Christ?
4. Read the following Scripture passages. List several characteristics of Christian behavior. These passages help people realize the need to repent and embrace a God-directed life. Discuss ways in which your congregation teaches and demonstrates these characteristics.
   • Galatians 5:22-23 (the fruits of the Spirit)
   • Matthew 5 (the Beatitudes)
   • 1 Corinthians 13 (the love chapter).

THE KINGDOM (REIGN) OF GOD

How do you talk to people about the reign of God? The announcement of the kingdom of God (God's reign) is another key point of the good news. For decades, many church and para-church organizations emphasized conversion "in order to get to heaven." By contrast, Jesus Christ's foundational message was, "Repent for the kingdom of God is near." His emphasis was on conversion that led to a change in behavior, thought, and action. These changes indicated that a person was choosing to live daily as a new citizen in God's reign (kingdom).

There is a marked difference between the two approaches. Salvation with heaven as the only goal has a distant future orientation. To emphasize a single future benefit can leave new Christians wondering what should be happening to and through them in the present. By contrast, salvation that invites us to be participants in God's kingdom and reign has a present orientation. The focus is on what is necessary to live in this new reality, right now.

Action Step:
Discuss the following with your pastor, leaders, and congregation:
1. How is the *present* reality of Christianity currently being shared through preaching, Christian education, and other ministries of our church?
2. Invite the church to complete a short questionnaire with the following questions on it:
   As a church:
   • Why do we exist?
   • What is our purpose?
   • What do we hope will happen to people as a result of coming to this church?
   • What difference are we going to make in the world?

Bear Witness

The early church embraced the Greek understanding of *bearing witness*, a legal term used to denote witness to facts, events, and truth. The validity of the act of bearing witness depended on two things: personal involvement and assurance of truth by the person bearing witness. People in the twenty-first century continue to look for this type of witness from Christians. The question is, How often do Christians provide a credible witness to others?

Rightly or wrongly, people who claim that they are Christians serve as a "living billboard for Christ." Mahatma Ghandi writes of *7 Deadly Sins*. The seventh sin is "worship *without* sacrifice," a prophetic statement that challenges the worship of a religion that asks nothing of its followers.

TO BEAR WITNESS: OLD TESTAMENT AND NEW TESTAMENT EXAMPLES

In the Old Testament, God bore witness of God's self through disclosure to humankind. The Bible references terms such as *tent of witness* or *ark of witness*. The tent was the place where God revealed God's divine presence to God's followers. The ark represented the record of God's self-disclosure.

God also called on the people of God to be witnesses to those who did not know God. The constant admonition to the people was "Fear not" or "Do not be afraid." It seems that people of all ages have had difficulty leaving their comfort zones to tell others about God.

In Acts and in the writings of the apostle John, *witness* took on a Christian distinction. *Witness* ordinarily meant to attest to facts or assert truths. The *Christian witness,* however, is more narrowly defined. Jesus commissioned the disciples to be his witnesses, attesting to what they had seen and had known about Jesus as the Christ. They were to assert to the truth of the facts of Jesus' life, his deeds, and his words. They were eyewitnesses who were to serve as heralds of divine truth. Paul, who was not an eyewitness, spoke of God bearing witness within him. In short, Paul had a testimony of personal spiritual transformation that was made evident by his life.

HOW CAN I BEAR WITNESS?

The key consideration in our Christian witness is the personal evidence that Christ is alive in us. People outside of Christianity want to know, *What difference has Christ made in our lives?* The validity of our witness depends on the reality of our personal interaction with Jesus Christ and our personal transformation by Jesus Christ. What process do you have in place that teaches people how to tell the story of their transformation through their Christian journey?

Action Step: Invite the pastor, leaders, and congregation to answer the following questions as a way of learning how to bear witness to Jesus Christ.

1. Think about your own Christian formation experience. Talk about a time in that formation process when you felt fully empowered by or in touch with the Holy Spirit, with God, with Jesus Christ. (This is THE story you would tell if you wanted to invite a reluctant participant to try this faith that you profess.)
2. Can you identify what made that moment, event, or experience possible? Who was present? Where were you? What contributed to this being a significant spiritual experience or transformative time?
3. Think of the power in this story and the influence of being discipled in faith. Next, imagine how you believe your local church will look in ten years. Then ask yourself, What one hope do you have for any ministry program or process that currently exists in your church to relate others to God and help seekers grow into spiritual maturity in Christ?
4. What one thing is your church currently doing effectively to bear witness to Christ to your community?
5. What is the most pressing community need that your church could address that would bear witness to Christ?

Proclaim

One major gospel message proclaimed by the early church was Jesus Christ himself. The early disciples had a confident belief and trust in Jesus Christ, the Messiah, who died and was resurrected from the grave.

The early disciples boldly retold the story of Jesus' earthly ministry, his deeds, his miracles, his teachings. These were oral people who never tired of telling and retelling the "old, old story of Jesus and his love." This constant telling and retelling of the story of Jesus Christ created a body of oral knowledge and awareness that circulated throughout the population. Stories in oral tradition serve as paperless receptacles for the storage and retrieval of information and for moral and spiritual instruction. There is a lesson that contemporary Christians can learn from this.

PREACHING AND BIBLE STORYTELLING

At an International Orality Network conference, an event dedicated to reaching oral learners with the gospel of Jesus Christ, a presenter noted that much of the preaching in Western Christianity is shared as exposition; that is, explanation about the Bible and Christian doctrine. This approach presumes two things: first, that most people prefer to receive information via explanation, lists, and logical arguments—characteristics of literate communication methods; second, that we are still living in *Christendom,* an age in which there was widespread Bible literacy.

In reality, the age of Christendom is over. Some refer to our present reality as either postmodern or post-Christian. This means that we can no longer presume that the listening audience has a basic familiarity with the Bible stories, such as Noah and the Ark, David and Goliath, Elijah and Elisha, or the feeding of the five thousand. Those Bible stories will have to be told in their entirety—again and again—to create an oral Bible within people, who can, in turn, retell those stories to friends and loved ones.

At the 2005 International Orality Conference, "Making Disciples of Oral Learners," Dr. Grant Lovejoy stated, "It seems certain that at least 60 percent of the total population worldwide are oral communicators by virtue of limited or nonexistent literacy skills." This means that we need to use oral communication or story rather than a literate style of presentation that relies heavily on lists, steps, and explanations.

Observe the communication vehicles that attract the attention of children, teens, and young adults—television, videos, video games, MP3 and CD players, and interactive Internet sites. There is little or no reading involved. All of the communication comes packaged as a video or audio story. The storyline communicates the message.

HOW DO WE PROCLAIM THE GOOD NEWS TODAY?

One simple thing to do is share with others the various things that Jesus said and did. According to some academics, we have now entered the third or fourth generation of biblically illiterate people in the United States. That means that sharing the stories of Jesus is more crucial now than ever before.

Action Step: Consider offering a Bible reading plan. Some churches invite people to read or listen to the Bible on cassette or CD throughout the year. Invite families to read Bible stories to their children from a children's Bible and invite the children to retell the stories in their own words. The Bible reading schedule could be coordinated with the preaching schedule and children's moments in worship. Include creative ways of *telling the story* in worship, such as:
- Bible dramas
- Bible storytelling
- Mime of a Bible story
- Liturgical dance/movement to interpret a story
- Scripture reading interspersed with music that underscores the text.

The Church Is a Come-*and*-Go Structure

C hurches of all sizes, locations, and ethnicities ask a common question, "How can we get more people to come to our church?" Shrinking membership rolls, neighborhoods in transition, and inadequate finances provide ample motivation for this request. However, viewing the church solely as a *come-structure* may be the wrong place to begin a discussion about evangelism. Think for a moment about what is involved with inviting an "outsider" to church.

Church Means . . .

What do you mean when you say *church*? Congregations in transitioning neighborhoods often express the desire to invite people from the community to church. The critical question is, "What is your definition of church?"

For example, let us presume that a historic "middle-class church" with dwindling membership is located in a transitioning neighborhood populated primarily by working-class persons from several different ethnic groups. Established populations and transient populations may have completely different understandings of what *church* is and how the church should function. In addition to being the place for spiritual and moral instruction, church — for marginalized people — historically has been a safe haven from oppression, a strategic planning center, an economic empowerment office, and a social gathering place. Even if a marginalized person did not attend church, he or she embraced some definition of what church stood for to him or her and the community.

HOW DOES YOUR CONGREGATION DEFINE CHURCH?

Before inviting people to come inside your local church consider the following types of questions.

When members of your congregation think of church, what comes to their minds? Trace the history of your local congregation. What significant events, ministries, and persons shaped your church's identity? How would you describe the *DNA* of your church culture; that is, who are you and what do you stand for? What does your local congregation call people to be and to do?

What, through Christ, does your local congregation have to offer the people in the surrounding community? Has your church developed a relationship with the community in any way? Has your congregation connected with the people who have *transitioned* into the neighborhood? Is your church aware of the major concerns of the people in the surrounding community? Is your congregation's concept of church similar to or different from the concept of church held by people in the community surrounding the church building? What do people in this community expect from a church? If your congregation were to invite people from the neighborhood who have vastly different understandings of *church*, who bears the responsibility of bridging the communication gap?

Action Step: Discuss the following questions with your pastor, leaders, and congregation.
1. If we discovered a *magic magnet* that would draw *outsiders* to our local church, what would they find when they arrived?
2. Ask congregation members to invite friends to church and have them provide feedback about your church's worship, preaching, music, and hospitality. Have members ask their friends to provide feedback about how they felt as first-time visitors to the Sunday worship experience.
3. Create a bulletin insert and ask members of your church to respond to the following questions:
   • What do you expect from a church?
   • What would make church meaningful for you (and/or your family)?
4. Ask several members of your church to conduct an informal survey with people in the neighborhood. Encourage them to ask questions, such as:
   • What do you expect from a church?
   • What would make church meaningful for you (and/or your family)?
   • What do you know about (*name of your church*) _____ United Methodist Church?"
5. Compare the answers from the members of your congregation and those from people in the neighborhood. Note the similarities and differences.

Pray for God's guidance in showing your congregation the unique gifts and graces that it has to offer to the community and how to build relationships with the people in the community.

WHAT REPUTATION DOES YOUR CHURCH HAVE?

Churches often hire consultants to "help them grow." In the first meeting, consultants often ask, "What reputation does your church have, or what is your church known for?" The point is to help the people discover what is unique about their local church. How might your congregation answer this question? When people state that they don't go to church because "it offers little of value" and that they simply "don't know why they don't go," it means that the local church has not made a positive impression on its community. How does the congregation express what it values?

Going Out Precedes Coming In

Effective evangelistic congregations concentrate both on inviting the people outside to "come" into the church and on equipping members inside to "go" out and reach people for Jesus Christ. It is helpful to think of the church as both a "come" and a "go" structure.

To develop a positive reputation outside the church facility, the people— who are the *real church*—must go out and engage other people in meaningful ways. The first step is deciding to do something meaningful to create a positive reputation *outside your church building*. The ministry of *going out* actually prepares you for the ministry of *coming in*.

Action Step:
Read the following examples. Then discuss what your local church is willing to do to create a positive reputation in the community for Christ.

1. Rudy and Juanita Rasmus, pastors of St. John's UMC in Houston, Texas, began with a handful of people and a goal of serving hurting people. After much prayer, they gathered a group of volunteers and renovated the former parsonage. They designed it to serve the homeless, hungry, and unemployed people who lived on the streets around the church facility. Furthermore, they decided to demystify the sanctuary so that homeless people would feel at ease coming into that space. They began the feeding ministry in the sanctuary.

The feeding ministry, called Bread of Life, has expanded. The homeless guests can wash and dry their clothes in the Bread of Life laundry. Health-care professionals offer basic health services, and group counseling is available for recovery from addiction. This church has a positive reputation in the community.

2. Steve Sjogren, in his book *101 Ways to Reach Your Community,* suggests having a "gasoline buy-down." This involves contacting a gas station manager and setting up a time (usually an hour or two) during which the gas price will be lowered—the church pays the difference. Members of the church provide service to the customers in the form of washing their windshields and—if time allows—checking the oil. While offering the service, church members explain that they are doing this as an expression of Christ's love. What type of reputation would this generate for a local church?

Encouraging people to come to church must be preceded by Christian disciples going out to engage the world with the love of Jesus Christ. What is your local church willing to do?

A BIBLICAL EXAMPLE
Throughout Jesus' earthly ministry he compelled and expected his disciples to reach out to others. The disciples were expected to partner with God to expand the kingdom or reign of God. In the Gospel accounts of Matthew, Mark, Luke, and John, each writer describes how Jesus sent out his disciples to make other disciples for him. The best known example is the Great Commission found in Matthew 28:16-20:

> Now the eleven disciples went to Galilee, to the mountain to which Jesus had directed them. When they saw him, they worshiped him; but some doubted. And Jesus came and said to them, "All authority in heaven and on earth has been given to me. Go therefore and make disciples of all nations, baptizing them in the name of the Father and of the Son and of the Holy Spirit, and teaching them to obey everything that I have commanded you. And remember, I am with you always, to the end of the age. (See also Mark 16:14-20; Luke 9:1-6; 24:44-49; John 20:19-23; Acts 1:6-8.)

Obeying the Great Commission is not one option among many for a congregation; it is at the very heart of the Christian enterprise. Christianity is a missionary, evangelizing faith.

The Process of Making Disciples
Think of your experience of coming to faith in God. What role did a congregation play? Think of how a congregation helped or hindered your Christian development. As a leader your role is to help shape a congregation that will reach out, welcome, and invite others to commit their lives to Christ. The congregation further helps to equip and empower people to live as Christian disciples.

IT TAKES A CONGREGATION TO MAKE A DISCIPLE
One way congregations make disciples is by developing an atmosphere that is welcoming, inviting, encouraging, and empowering. Two major factors in this process are attentiveness to God and faith development of every person in the congregation. Other factors are trust, generational and ethnic inclusiveness, hospitality, and spiritual leaders—lay and clergy—who equip disciples for ministry in the world.

Evangelism is, at its heart, sharing faith with others, particularly with those who are unchurched or disconnected, and inviting them to follow

Jesus Christ as Christian disciples. Effective congregations develop a disciple-making system that welcomes and invites, equips, and sends disciples forth in ministry. Growing congregations receive new persons on profession of their faith not just transfers from other churches.

Job Description

As a leader of the evangelism ministry of your church, you have various responsibilities. These include:

1. Serving as team leader for those assigned to work with you, guiding the work of the team, helping them to work from a biblical and theological foundation, creating work space in which Christian faith formation happens, planning agendas, presiding at meetings, and representing the ministry of evangelism in meetings of the church council and charge conference.
2. Working with the pastor and team in assessing your congregation's vital statistics that relate to growth, such as membership (paying particular attention to professions of faith) and attendance trends, as well as the way in which new people are received into the congregation and empowered for ministry.
3. Promoting evangelism as a core value of each ministry of the church.
4. Envisioning what God's will for the congregation's future might be and setting goals that are consistent with that vision.
5. Developing a plan for an overall evangelism strategy and system that reaches out to persons, welcomes them into the congregation, relates them to God, and equips and empowers them for ministry.
6. Implementing your plan.

How to Start

BUILD THE EVANGELISM MINISTRY TEAM

Evangelism is ultimately the work of the Holy Spirit. Start building your team with prayer. The committee on nominations and leadership development may help to identify team members, though you may need to recruit or add members yourself. Your pastor can assist you with suggestions. At your first meeting determine a time of day when team members will be in prayer for one another and for the development of a common vision for the congregation's evangelistic ministry.

Build a team with persons committed to the ministry of evangelism. A team differs from a committee in that a team is personally involved. A team is aligned around a single purpose. Depending on the size of the congregation, a team should consist of a workable number—no fewer than five and no more than a dozen. Your team should represent a cross section of the congregation. If you do not currently have an evangelism team, you might want to include as members your lay leader, any lay speakers in the congregation, a youth and at least one young adult.

Agree on a reading schedule and include this Guideline on it. Work through the action steps included in this Guideline with your pastor, team, and as much as possible, with other key church leaders and members of the congregation.

Read the Bible for your own spiritual formation and for models of evangelism and faith sharing. Important passages in this regard include:
• Matthew 9:35–10:23 (call of the disciples)
• Luke 4:16-21 (Jesus' sermon in the synagogue)
• Luke 8:26-39 (Jesus' expulsion of unclean spirits)
• Luke 10:1-20 (mission of the seventy)
• Luke 10:25-37 (parable of the good Samaritan)
• Luke 15 (parables of the lost sheep, coin, and son)
• John 1:35-51 (call of Jesus' first disciples)
• John 20:19-31 (post-resurrection appearance of Jesus).

Read the Book of Acts for a description of the missionary evangelism of the early church and the way that a vital church reaches out to new groups of people.

ASSESS CURRENT REALITY
First, assess the strengths and weaknesses of the current ministry efforts. How does your church presently reach out and welcome persons into the life of the church? How effective are these activities? What are the results? You can measure these by assembling the reportable vital statistics of the last five to ten years: membership, worship and Sunday school attendance, and faithfulness in stewardship. If this data is not readily available, check the conference journal. The statistical pages include every church's membership growth, average worship size, and Sunday school attendance. *The most important statistics concern the number of people joining the church on profession of faith, the net growth or decline each year, and the average weekly attendance at worship, Sunday school, and other small groups.* Statistics related to giving can also be helpful to measure growth in discipleship. Is giving on the rise? What is the percentage of giving to mission projects in and through the local congregation? Compile the information from

the statistics and determine where the strengths and weaknesses are in your local church. Celebrate your strengths. Ask *why questions* about both your strengths and weaknesses. Keep asking why until root causes are determined. Then, devise a plan of action that builds on your strengths and successes to improve the vitality of your congregation. This should help improve the areas of weakness as well.

Another important piece of information concerns the numbers of members who are considered inactive or marginal. Who are they? Why are they inactive? Who might be able to reconcile with them on behalf of the church? The percentage of marginal members should be low if a viable discipleship system is in place and active in your local church.

Obtaining demographic data about your community is helpful. Your conference office may have such information for your community. If that office doesn't have it, you may contact the Office of Research of the General Board of Global Ministries directly, which can supply this information. (See the Resources section for details.) From these findings, you will be able to determine the numbers and age groupings of people in your community.

When these data are assembled, spend enough meeting time to analyze the material prayerfully. What is God saying to you through it?

Is your church good at welcoming strangers? Various studies show that between 75 and 90 percent of new members affiliated with their present congregation because of a *relational factor*. Check this out with your ad hoc team of new members. How did they make friendships? What is the congregation doing to encourage this development? What could be improved?

Be objective. The goal is to learn whether you have a working discipleship system in place, not to assign credit or blame or to rationalize the data.

See "Our Church's Hospitality to Visitors" on page 26 and discover how friendly the church really is. For more information on discerning the vitality and direction for your congregation, go to www.cvindicator.com.

DEVELOP A SHARED VISION

In *The Fifth Discipline,* Peter Senge tells us, "Few, if any, forces in human affairs are as powerful as shared vision" (See Resources.) Vision is essential to growth. *A process for developing a shared vision among an evangelism ministry team should begin with prayer.* Spend time in team meetings on the personal vision or hopes that people have for their church. Who are the people left out or ignored in your community? What one thing could the church do that would make the most difference? The vision must be shared with the church council and other teams in order for an integrated vision to develop, which will empower the congregation to move forward.

ESTABLISH A PLAN

It is common wisdom that when we fail to plan, we plan to fail! Remember that the mission of the church is to make disciples for Jesus Christ. Vital, growing congregations will have a comprehensive plan for evangelism. Your task is to lead the evangelism ministry team in designing your congregation's discipleship system.

A discipleship system needs to focus on these areas: *welcoming, incorporating persons into the congregation, and equipping and sending them out as disciples of Jesus Christ.* The following pages will assist you and your team in developing a comprehensive plan for evangelism.

SET YOUR PLAN INTO MOTION

Action causes change. Do not spend too much time meeting and planning. Move quickly to action. Your whole discipleship plan does not need to be in place before you begin a part of it that your team believes is essential. For example, your team could choose to study personal faith sharing and could covenant to begin by each team member's filling out a F-R-A-N Plan (see "Implement Your Evangelism Plan") and agreeing to be held accountable by the team.

Team leader, remember two things: keep cool and have fun. As a friend of mine likes to say it, if joy is missing in the work of evangelism, only the "news" section of the "good news" is present!

Implement Your Evangelism Plan

a ccording to *The Book of Discipline of The United Methodist Church,* the mission of each church is "to make disciples of Jesus Christ for the transformation of the world" (¶120; see also ¶¶121-122). Congregations need not spend time in defining the church's mission. It is already stated. The primary task of the church in fulfilling that mission is to:
  • reach out to people wherever they are and receive them as they are
  • relate them to God through Jesus Christ
  • nurture and equip them for Christian discipleship, and

• send them out into the community to be the church in the family, the neighborhood, the community, and the world.

As you read, put a star by the ideas in the following categories you want to explore with your team and with the congregation.

Reach Out and Receive

INVITATION AND WELCOME
A widely held perception in US culture is that church property is private property and that churches are for members only. To change this perception, congregations must become more intentional in invitation and welcome. To whom does your church send its newsletter? To members only? What does that say? Be sure to include recent visitors, families of church school children, and—if you can get their addresses—persons who attend community groups in your church. Consider the following possibilities.

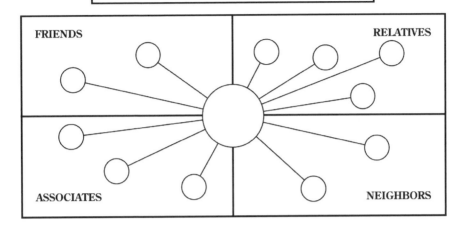

Give church members a copy of the above diagram or the *Personal F-R-A-N Plan: A Ministry* leaflet available through Discipleship Resources. The F-R-A-N Plan helps people identify friends (F), relatives (R), associates (A), and neighbors (N) who are not practicing Christians. Ask your members to commit to pray for these unchurched and disconnected friends each day and to invite them to church for worship or some other congregational event.

BRING-A-FRIEND SUNDAY
Set one Sunday each month and ask your members to bring a friend. Have greeters at the door and design the worship experience so that visitors will feel welcome. Make sure the worship bulletin is "user-friendly." As examples: Print the Lord's Prayer. List the page number of Scripture readings from pew Bibles, and so forth. Ask your pastor to preach something very basic and relevant to unchurched people on that Sunday to help visitors understand what United Methodist Christians believe. The goal is to get United Methodists to be invitational until every Sunday becomes "bring a friend Sunday." Recruit other congregations in your community to go along with the project and do joint promotion in the local newspaper. Be especially aware of inviting others when Igniting Ministries media campaigns are done in your area. (These are sponsored through United Methodist Communications and your local area churches.)

ESTABLISH RELATIONSHIPS
Faith-sharing is relational evangelism. Provide opportunities for building relationships, such as offering tutoring or mentoring programs. Invite

members to establish relationships with people through fitness centers or conversations with people at Little League games, and so on.

VISIT YOUR VISITORS
Make a follow-up visit, phone call, or mailing to visitors. *Studies indicate that the sooner a response is made, the better the chances that the person will affiliate with the congregation. The same studies show that a visit by a layperson or a lay couple is most effective.* Consider the cultural expectations in your community. Some areas expect unannounced visits; others are repelled by them. When in doubt, call for an appointment before visiting.

TELL YOUR STORY
The best advertising is always word of mouth, but there are innovative ways of telling your story. Advertise where unchurched people look. Consider an ad in the real estate or obituary section; leave flyers under the windshield wipers on cars in supermarket parking lots on Saturday mornings. Many churches have an artist in their membership who could design a Christmas postcard to be sent to all visitors in the past year who haven't affiliated. Easter is another time when people are more conscious of their spiritual needs.

MAKING MEMBERSHIP MORE MEANINGFUL
Studies of congregational life reveal that as many as one-half of those who join churches become inactive in their first year of membership. Find ways to assimilate new members. Remember that the mission is to make disciples, not members. Visitors should be welcomed as guests. Members need to feel like members of the family.

When new members are graciously and intentionally assimilated, they
- continue to grow spiritually through small groups
- have at least seven personal friends in the congregation
- have identified gifts and callings and are exercising them
- understand, identify with, and support the mission and vision of the congregation
- are excited about the congregation and naturally invite friends, family members, and neighbors to become disciples of Christ.

To assist in this process, assign sponsors or fellowship friends to each new member, person, or family. These "shepherds" would help introduce newcomers to other members of the congregation and Sunday school class leaders and invite them to fellowship events.

Design and manage, under the pastor's direction, a plan whereby persons interested in exploring Christian faith or church membership could have opportunities to learn about Christianity, United Methodism, and the mission and ministry of your own congregation.

Assist newcomers in the congregation in identifying their own visions, gifts, and callings. Evidence exists that each person has to be connected to a congregation in three ways to stay connected: a worship connection, a fellowship connection, and a service connection.

Keep your eyes open! Maintain records to ensure that members are promptly missed and contacted if they begin to drift away. People feel important when they are missed! Studies of inactive people show that, in many cases, people will test out becoming inactive to see whether "anyone would miss me."

Relate People to God

Your congregation's spiritual life is nurtured in a variety of practices and settings: worship, personal devotions, private and group study of the Bible, personal faith sharing, small groups for learning and practicing the spiritual disciplines, discovering and using spiritual gifts, and serving others. *The goal is a personal relationship with God through Jesus Christ.*

It is important for the ministry team to spend time at each meeting in intentional spiritual formation. Ministry area members might share their own experiences of being formed in Christ. Ask questions like, "Who have been the two or three most spiritually influential persons in your life?" and "What one circumstance has influenced you the most in your spiritual journey?"

You might consider having a spiritual life emphasis sometime in the "great fifty days" between Easter and Pentecost. If the Walk to Emmaus is active in your area, it can be a valuable resource for helping people relate to God. You might consider sponsoring and supporting a person to attend the Academy for Spiritual Formation, sponsored by the Upper Room.

Nurture and Equip People for Christian Discipleship

TURNING UP THE THERMOSTAT

There is a difference between a thermometer and a thermostat. A thermometer registers the temperature; the thermostat changes it. The climate of a congregation is most affected by attitudes and relationships within the congregation. Attitudes and relationships are affected by people's continual spiritual renewal.

John Wesley promoted a personal and congregational lifestyle focused on what was called the means of grace (see below). Practicing these means of grace helps us to sense Christ's presence.

MEANS OF GRACE

Works of Piety
(Personal Holiness)

Works of Mercy
(Social Holiness)

- Prayer (private and family)
- Public worship
- The Lord's Supper
- Reading and studying Scripture
- Christian conferencing
- Fasting or abstinence
- Peacemaking
- Regular participation in a small group for spiritual nurture and accountability

- Feeding the hungry
- Clothing the naked
- Caring for the sick
- Visiting the jails and prisons
- Sheltering the homeless
- Welcoming the stranger
- Acting for the common good

In pursuing such means of grace, vital congregations commonly do three things: *they promote (1) the small group experience, (2) a congregation-wide, focused Bible study, and (3) personal involvement in ministry and mission.*

You may want to consider offering your members some of the small group experiences below (see Resources).

- *Transforming Evangelism* is an overview of a Wesleyan approach to evangelism that may be used as a six-week study for small groups.

- *Witness* is a small group study that helps individuals share faith and invite others into the body of Christ. A second part of the study helps change the climate and culture of the congregation to be one of "witness."

- DISCIPLE Bible Study groups have also been found effective for changing the congregational climate. These groups gain the benefits of the small group experience while also having the possibility of aligning a congregation around a sharply focused Bible study.

- *Companions in Christ* is a twenty-four week small group experience in which persons learn to share their faith.

Send Out Disciples into the Community

Jesus announced that he had come "not to be served but to serve" (Matthew 20:28). A disciple of Jesus is, first of all, a servant. Service is the heartbeat of discipleship. "As the Father has sent me, so I send you," says Jesus to the church today (John 20:21). Discipleship is being sent forth into homes, schools, workplaces, and communities at large to serve with the gifts of God. The possibilities of service are beyond counting in the ministry area of every congregation. Doing acts of mercy is one of the ways we tell the Christian story.

Your team can assist your pastor in helping members of the congregation discover and identify their gifts for ministry, including their gifts and graces through service evangelism. Invite people to serve, for example, at a food bank, a Habitat for Humanity project, an after-school tutoring program, a Meals on Wheels program, or a prison ministry.

Consider the possibility of assisting in the establishment of a new congregation, which is the most effective evangelism strategy. Ask your district superintendent if there is a new church development planned in your area and volunteer to help.

EXAMINE YOUR EFFECTIVENESS

How can we know if we are being effective in our ministries? Former Bishop David J. Lawson suggested asking five questions:

1. Are persons growing in relationship to God through participating in our congregations? Are they freely yielding increasing portions of their life to the influence of Christ's teachings?
2. Are persons growing in their knowledge of Scripture, the wisdom of the Christian Movement, and the history of our church? Are they moving beyond an elementary level of understanding?
3. Are persons giving evidence of increased Christian commitment by the way they live?
4. Are persons growing in compassionate world citizenship, actively learning about and responding to needs of others, and finding practical ways to express membership in this global United Methodist Church?
5. Are persons viewing our congregations as supportive centers of excitement and joy? Are we inventing new approaches to worship and programming that are responsive to the needs of unchurched persons living within our assigned parishes? Are we discovering new ways of learning what these needs and interests are?

(David J. Lawson, in *Discipleship Dateline*, November 1993, General Board of Discipleship.)

Our Church's Hospitality to Visitors
(10 points for each Yes, except numbers 5 and 6)

1 Does the church have ample parking? Yes ____ No ____
2. Is there a specific part of the parking lot designated for visitor parking? Yes ____ No ____
3. Are there greeters in the parking lot? Yes ____ No ____
4. Are there adequate signs directing visitors to parking, restrooms, nursery, the sanctuary, and Sunday school? Yes ____ No ____
5. Do greeters: (*5 points each*)
   a. Offer a friendly welcome? Yes ____ No ____
   b. Introduce visitors by name to the usher? Yes ____ No ____
6. Do ushers: (*2 points each*)
   a. Help visitors find a seat? Yes ____ No ____
   b. Provide each visitor with a bulletin? Yes ____ No ____
   c. Introduce visitors to other worshipers? Yes ____ No ____
   d. Give each visitor a visitor badge, ribbon, or cross? Yes ____ No ____
   e. Help a visitor find the nursery (if needed)? Yes ____ No ____
7. Do the members wear nametags? Yes ____ No ____
8. Are visitors given the opportunity to register their attendance (name, address, phone, and other information) on a registration pad? Yes ____ No ____
9. Is the congregation alert to give a friendly welcome to visitors? Yes ____ No ____
10. Does the pastor welcome visitors during the worship service? (*Deduct 5 points if visitors are asked to stand or raise their hand.*) Yes ____ No ____
11. Do members get the names of visitors and introduce them to other members? Yes ____ No ____
12. Are visitors invited for coffee or other refreshments (before or after the service)? Yes ____ No ____
13. If you have a "coffee time," are there persons designated to spot new people and to introduce and involve them in conversation with other members? Yes ____ No ____

14. Does someone offer to take each visitor on
a tour of the church building?   Yes ____ No ____
15. Is every visitor invited to a Sunday
school class?   Yes ____ No ____
16. Are visitors provided an opportunity
to meet the pastor?   Yes ____ No ____
17. Does someone invite each visitor to be his
or her guest or go with that person to
a church function?   Yes ____ No ____
18. Are visitors invited to a membership
orientation class?   Yes ____ No ____
19. Does someone call on each visitor within
forty-eight hours?   Yes ____ No ____
20. Is your Sunday school and small group
system being used to train and equip
members to "share faith," reach out to
people, and welcome newcomers
into the fellowship?   Yes ____ No ____

Key for Tabulation

(10 points for each question, except 5 and 6. Total your score!)

0–24   Church hostile toward visitors.
25–49   Tolerant (cool) toward visitors.
50–74   Visiting is permitted, but not encouraged.
75–99   Lukewarm toward visitors.
100–124   Visitors are casually prepared for.
125–149   Visiting is encouraged.
150–174   Visitors are important and prepared for.
175–200   Visitors are treated like honored guests and potential members
          and will know you want them as part of your fellowship.

"Our Church's Hospitality to Visitors," from *Evangelism Ministries
Planning Handbook* by Suzanne Braden, Discipleship Resources 1987;
questionnaire developed by Rick Kirchoff.

RESOURCES

** Indicates our top picks

WEB RESOURCES
- **The General Board of Discipleship Evangelism Website** www.gbod.org/evangelism/ or www.umcevangelism.org
- **Evangelistic Preaching Helps**—aids evangelistic sermon preparation.
- **Offering Christ Today**—provides tips on evangelism and suggested resources.
- **Stories for Survivors**—Bible stories for survivors of disaster.

- **Chrysalis:** www.upperroom.org/chrysalis for young adults and teens

- **Church Vitality Indicator:** www.cvindicator.com. A web-based tool for congregational assessment, discernment of areas of influence and vitality, and helps for how to find the focus area for greater vitality.

- **The Faith Sharing Initiative**—a strategy for training laity to share their faith. www.gbod.org/evangelism/fsparticipants.pdf. For training contact Rev. Royal Speidel (rspeidel1@comcast.net)

- **The Faith Sharing Initiative (Spanish Version)** http://www.gbod.org/evangelism/elcompromiso.pdf

- **The Foundation for Evangelism:** www.evangelize.org

- **Igniting Ministries:** www.ignitingministry.org

- **National Association of United Methodist Evangelists:** www.naume.org Contact Charles Whittle at P.O. Box 24241, Fort Worth, TX 76124. Phone: 817-451-4408 Fax: 817-451-4409; e-mail: charleswhittle@juno.com.

- **Walk to Emmaus, The:** www.upperroom.org/emmaus

MULTICULTURAL EVANGELISM
- **Many Faces, One Church,** by Ernest S. Lyght, Glory Dharmaraj, Jacob Dharmaraj (Nashville: Abingdon, 2006. ISBN 978-0-687-49445-3).

• **The New Faces of Christianity: Believing the Bible in the Global South,* by Philip Jenkins (New York: Oxford University Press, 2006. ISBN 978-0-195-30065-9).

• **The Next Christendom,* by Philip Jenkins (New York: Oxford University Press, 2007. ISBN 978-0-19-518307-8).

• *Whose Religion Is Christianity?: The Gospel Beyond the West,* by Lamin Sanneh (Grand Rapids: Wm. B. Eerdmans, 2003. ISBN 0-8028-2164-2).

SPANISH LANGUAGE EVANGELISM RESOURCES
(Discipleship Resources titles are available through Upper Room Ministries www.UpperRoom.org/bookstore, 1-800-972-0433)

• ***El plan personal de Alcance,* translated and adapted by Lía Icaza-Willetts (Nashville: Discipleship Resources, 2001. ISBN 978-0-88177-358-3).

• ***La congregación que comparte su fe,* by Roger K. Swanson and Shirley F. Clement; translated and adapted by José A. Malavé García (Nashville: Discipleship Resources, 2001. ISBN 978-0-88177-312-5).

• *Las 10 preguntas más frecuentes entre los nuevos Cristianos,* by Peter Harrington, translated by Martha E. Rovira-Raber (Nashville: Discipleship Resources, 2001. ISBN 978-0-88177-330-9).

• *Libertad a los cautivos,* by Vanessa Alers (Nashville: Discipleship Resources, 2002. ISBN 978-0881773378).

• ***Módulo III: Elementos esenciales en la facilitación en la educatión Christiana,* by Ada Chong, Lucrecia Cotto, Hildelisa Ordaz, Marigene Chamberlain, Saúl Trinidad, y Alma Perez (Nashville: Discipleship Resources, 2006. ISBN 978-0-88177-453-5).

• *Nuestro liderato como evangelistas,* by Roger K. Swanson and Shirley F. Clement, translated by Ada Chong (Nashville: Discipleship Resources, 2005. ISBN 978-0-88177-432-0).

• *Sendas hacia Cristo:*
    Hacia una nueva vida en Cristo, por Mitchell Williams translated by Rev. Humberto Casanova (Nashville: *Discipleship Resources,* 2005. ISBN 978-0-88177-450-2).

• *Mi jornada de fe con Cristo,* por Wesley S. K. Daniel (Nashville: Discipleship Resources, 2007. ISBN 978-0-88177-524-2).
• *Mis dones en Cristo,* por Craig Kennet Miller (Nashville: Discipleship Resources, 2007. ISBN 978-0-88177-523-5).
• *Nueva vida, nuevos hábitos,* por Safiyah Fosua (Nashville: Discipleship Resources, 2007. ISBN 978-0-88177-522-8).
• *Guías de Estudio Para los librillos de Sendas hacia Cristo* www.upperrom.org/bookstore. Avaiable as PDF download with each title.

EVANGELISM RESOURCES

• *Ancient Future Evangelism: Making Your Church a Faith-Forming Community,* by Robert E. Webber (Grand Rapids: Baker, 2003. ISBN 978-0-80109-160-5).

• *Biblical Perspectives on Evangelism,* by Walter Brueggemann (Nashville: Abingdon, 1993. ISBN 978-0-687-41233-4).

• **Church for the Unchurched,* by George G. Hunter III (Nashville: Abingdon, 1996. ISBN 978-0-687-27732-2).

• *Demographic data of your church and community* are available through the Office of Research, General Board of Global Ministries. 212-870-3840. www.new.gbgm-umc.org/about/um/org/research/

• *Evangelism After Christendom: The Theology and Practice of Christian Witness,* by Bryan Stone (Grand Rapids: Brazos Press, 2006. ISBN 978-1-58743-194-4).

• *The Fifth Discipline: The Art and Practice of the Learning Organization,* by Peter M. Senge (New York: Doubleday/Currency, 2006. ISBN 9780385517256).

• *Leading Beyond the Walls,* by Adam Hamilton (Nashville: Abingdon Press, 2002. ISBN 978-0-687-06415-1).

• *The Pathways to Christ Pamphlet Series:* Nashville: Discipleship Resources (Also in Spanish and Korean)

Begin with Jesus, by Mitchell Williams (2005. ISBN 978-0-8817-7446-7).

• *Understanding My Journey with Christ,* by Wesley S. K. Daniel (2007. ISBN 978-0-8817-7447-4).

• *Learning New Habits,* by Safiyah Fosua (2007. ISBN 978-0-8817-7448-1).

• *Gifted in Christ,* by Craig Kennet Miller (2007. ISBN 978-0-8817-7449-8). Free Online Leaders Guide Available: umcevangelism.org

• *Radical Outreach: The Recovery of Apostolic Ministry and Evangelism,* by George G. Hunter III (Nashville: Abingdon, 2003. ISBN 978-0-687-07441-9).

• **Transforming Evangelism,* by Henry H. Knight, III and F. Douglas Powe, Jr. (Nashville: Discipleship Resources, 2006. ISBN 978-0-88177-485-6).

• **Your Church Can Thrive: Making the Connections That Build Healthy Congregations,* by Harold Percy (Nashville: Abingdon Press, 2003. ISBN 978-0-687-02256-4).

SMALL GROUP AND DISCIPLE FORMATION RESOURCES
• **Accountable Discipleship,* by Steven W. Manskar (Nashville: Discipleship Resources, 2000. ISBN 978-0-88177-339-2).

• *Beyond the Roll Book,* by Diana L. Hynson and Scott J. Jones (Nashville: Abingdon Press, 2006. ISBN 978-0-68764-140-6).

• **Charting the Course,* by Teresa Gilbert, Patty Johansen, Jay Regennitter with John P. Gilbert (Nashville: Discipleship Resources, 2007. ISBN 978-0-88177-507-5).

• *The Church in Many Houses,* by Steve Cordle (Nashville: Abingdon, 2005. ISBN 978-0-68732-579-5).

• **Deepening Your Effectiveness,* by Dan Glover and Claudia Lavy (Nashville: Discipleship Resources, 2006. ISBN 978-0-88177-475-7).

HOSPITALITY/WELCOMING RESOURCES
• *Making Room: Recovering Hospitality as a Christian Tradition,* by Christine D. Pohl (Grand Rapids: Wm. B. Eerdmans, 1999. ISBN 978-0-80284-431-6).

• *The Race to Reach Out,* by Douglas T. Anderson and Michael J. Coyner (Nashville: Abingdon, 2004. ISBN 978-0-68706-668-1).

FAITH SHARING

- DISCIPLE Bible Study, available in four phases. Contact: Cokesbury Seminars, 800-251-8591. www.cokesbury.com; then Search *disciple*.

- *Faith-Sharing: Dynamic Christian Witnessing by Invitation,* by H. Eddie Fox and George Morris (Nashville: Discipleship Resources, 1996. ISBN 978-0-88177-158-9) & Faith-Sharing Video Kit (ISBN 978-0-88177-207-4).

- *The Faith-Sharing New Testament and Psalms* (Nashville: Cokesbury, in cooperation with Thomas Nelson, Inc., 1996. ISBN 0-687-06716-9).

- *The Faith-Sharing Congregation,* by Roger K. Swanson and Shirley F. Clement (Nashville: Discipleship Resources, 1996. ISBN 978-0-88177-153-4).

- *Personal F.R.A.N. Plan* (Nashville: Discipleship Resources. Wallet-size leaflets for praying and faith sharing. ISBN 978-0-88177-259-3).

- *Witness: Workbook and Journal Set,* by Ronald K. Crandall (Nashville: Discipleship Resources, 2007. ISBN 978-088177-493-1).

For additional resources, check with your annual conference office.

Guidelines Resources

General Board of Church and Society, 202-488-5600; *www.umc-gbcs.org;* Service Center, 1-800-967-0880

General Board of Discipleship, 877-899-2780; *www.gbod.org;* Discipleship Resources, 1-800-972-0433; *www.discipleshipresources.org;* The Upper Room, 1-800-972-0433; *www.upperroom.org*

General Board of Global Ministries, 1-800-UMC-GBGM (1-800-862-4246); 212-870-3600; *http://gbgm-umc.org; email: info@gbgm-umc.org*

General Board of Higher Education and Ministry, 615-340-7400; *www.gbhem.org*

General Board of Pension and Health Benefits, 847-869-4550; *www.gbophb.org*

General Commission on Archives and History, 973-408-3189; *www.gcah.org*

General Commission on Christian Unity and Interreligious Concerns, 212-749-3553; *www.gccuic-umc.org*

General Commission on Religion & Race, 202-547-2271, *www.gcorr.org, info@gcorr.org*

General Commission on the Status & Role of Women, 1-800-523-8390; *www.gcsrw.org*

General Commission on United Methodist Men, 615-340-7145, *www.gcumm.org;* Office of Civic Youth Serving Agencies/Scouting, 615-340-7145; *www.gcumm.org*

General Council on Finance and Administration, 1-866-367-4232; *www.gcfa.org*

United Methodist Communications, 615-742-5400; *www.umcom.org;* EcuFilm, 1-888-346-3862; InfoServ, 1-800-251-8140; Interpreter, 615-742-5107; *www.interpretermagazine.org*

The United Methodist Publishing House, 615-749-6000, *www.umph.org;* Curric-U-Phone, 1-800-251-8591; Cokesbury, 1-800-672-1789; *www.cokesbury.com*

Download the free training booklet, "A Guide to the Guidelines: A Workshop to Orient Leaders to the Guidelines" from *www.cokesbury.com.*

For additional resources, contact your Annual Conference office.

GUIDELINES

2009-2012

"The mission of the Church is to make disciples of Jesus Christ for the transformation of the world. Local churches provide the most significant arena through which disciple-making occurs" (*The Book of Discipline of The United Methodist Church*).

EVANGELISM

Evangelism is vital to the disciple-making process because it is a primary ministry of sharing the Good News of Jesus Christ. Evangelism is more than just one individual talking about faith; it is a ministry of the whole church that develops a church "lifestyle" of welcome, invitation, and support. In this Guideline, look for this and more:

- A biblical and theological basis for evangelism
- The basics of evangelism ministry
- Building an evangelism ministry team
- Assessing your church's hospitality to visitors
- Equipping people for service

The twenty-six Guidelines cover church leadership areas including *Church Council, Pastor,* and *Lay Leader/Lay Member;* the administrative areas of *Finance* and *Trustees;* and ministry areas focused on nurture, outreach, and witness including *Worship, Evangelism, Stewardship,* and more. The complete set of Guidelines (ISBN 9780687647224) includes a CD-ROM with searchable files of all twenty-six Guidelines as well as a workshop to introduce the Guidelines to your ministry team, oversize charts and worksheets, and more.

The Guidelines are available from Cokesbury in sets or individually.

Church Council	Communications	Children's Ministries
Small Membership Church	Church Historian	Youth Ministries
Pastor	Trustees	Adult Ministries
Lay Leader/Lay Member	Finance	Family Ministries
Nominations and Leadership	Worship	Youth Serving Ministry
Development	Evangelism	Women's Ministries
Pastor-Parish Relations	Stewardship	Men's Ministries
Advocates for Inclusiveness	Mission	Church & Society
Small Group Ministries	Christian Education	Higher Education & Campus Ministry

ISBN-13: 978-0-687-64921-1

90000

9 780687 649211

Cokesbury

Resources for the Christian Journey

1-800-672-1789
www.cokesbury.com

THE CHRISTMAS THIEF

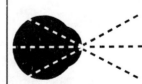

This Large Print Book carries the
Seal of Approval of N.A.V.H.